Tacenda Literary Magazine

2015 Edition

EDITOR-IN-CHIEF
Alexa Marie Kelly

CONSULTING EDITOR
Robert Johnson

COVER DESIGN
Carla Mavaddat

TEXT DESIGN
Sonia Tabriz

BleakHouse Publishing
2015

Ward Circle Building 254
American University
Washington, DC 20016
www.BleakHousePublishing.com

Robert Johnson - Editor & Publisher
Sonia Tabriz - Managing Editor
Liz Calka - Creative Director

Shirin Karimi - Senior Creative Consultant
Daniella Decker - Art Director
Carla Mavaddat -- Curator

Casey Chiappetta - Chief Operating Officer
Alexa Marie Kelly - Chief Editorial Officer
Emily Dalgo - Chief Development Officer
Rachel Ternes - Chief Creative Officer

Copyright © 2015 by Robert Johnson

All rights reserved. No part of this book shall be reproduced or transmitted in any form or by any means, electronic, mechanical, magnetic, photographic including photocopying, recording or by any information storage and retrieval system, without prior written permission of the publisher. No patent liability is assumed with respect to the use of the information contained herein. Although every precaution has been taken in the preparation of this book, the publisher and author assume no responsibility for errors or omissions. Neither is any liability assumed for damages resulting from the use of the information contained herein.

ISBN: 978-0-9961162-0-6

Printed in the United States of America

A Note From the Editors

TACENDA: n., pronounced ta'KEN'da
'things better left unsaid'

BleakHouse may have a misleading name.

We publish Tacenda Literary Magazine not to celebrate what's bleak but to expose it, so that we can foster hope for the future. Each page of Tacenda 2015 exposes our criminal justice system. Some of our authors have been entangled in the system. Some are still in prison. All of our artists have thought about the experience of men and women behind bars. The men and women we label criminals but often forget to label as human.

Tacenda recognizes humanity, its forms and disfigurements.

Together, these original works of literature challenge popular notions of crime. They shed light on what it means to be a prisoner, and ultimately, what it means to be human.

Thank you to our writers, especially those writing from prison cells (real or in our hearts and minds.) Thank you to Professor Robert Johnson, our consulting editor and mentor. You inspire us. You encourage everyone you know.

Thank you reader for your continued support and open mind.

    Alexa Marie Kelly
    Editor-in-Chief

Table of Contents

The Game	Lorena Lipe	5
This Game Ain't No Game	Daniel "Vito" Johnson	7
38.7442° N, 90.3053° W	Mikala Rempe	11
Dear Society	Christine Hwang	13
The Crowd	Sofia Crutchfield	15
Alternative Endings	Brian Medich	17
The Ride In	Jason Russin	19
The Things They Carried	Maggie Brennan	20
The Mural	Grace Austin	22
Doorway to Oblivion	Anne Scherer	24
Contained	Ainsley Bruno	25
Species x	Lorena Lipe	26
Math	Shyla Bergin	28
The Beat	Jason Russin	29
The Dance	Daniella Sklarz	30
You Are My Catalyst	Emily Dalgo	31
I Know Pain	D'angelo	32
Pain on Paper	Elijahwon Watts	33
Dear Anybody	Christine Hwang	34

Isolation	Anne Scherer	36
Unsociable	Garrett Hubbell	38
Crocus	Alfred " Spoken Truth" Dearing	39
Bloom Grown From a Crack in the Wall	Beverly Jaynes	41
Heat Waves	Jason Russin	42
The Weather in Solitary	Brian Medich	43
Drown	Marisa Fein	44
Cherry Red	John Raley	52
Drunks: Losers	Rick Lyon	53
Audacity	G. Leaks	54
No More Innocence	DJ	56
Realizations	Ainsley Bruno	57
Phone Calls	Aiden Banks	58
Depression Is Loneliness Always	Emily Dalgo	61
Where the Forgotten Wait	Maggie Brennan	62
Another Love Song	Michael Drummond	64
Stranger	Ian Luciano	65
Her Eyes	Vlada Grayton	67
Ghost Dad	Juan	68

One Decision, Ten Seconds	Jen Holthaus	69
Knocked Up	Vlada Grayton	71
The Duty of Leaving Imprints	Anthony Winn	73
A Way Out	Tatiana Shanique Laing	75
Forgive Me	DJ	79
Second Chances Aren't Given, They're Earned	Rufus Avery	80
Still Walking... Mile #1	G. Leaks	87
Last Rites Primeval	Robert Johnson	89
About the Editors & Authors		90

The Game
Lorena Lipe

I thought that if I played it
good and right,
I could win. That if I
followed their religion
blindly, and without fight, I would
somehow
make it out of here alive
with my scars as the only proof
of the battles I fought. It seems, however,
I was not the one to act
sacrilegiously.

My life is not a consolation prize
and my soul cannot be
pawned off like a gold watch
with scratches to prove its wear.

Maybe it is my inherent optimism
that led me to believe that there is
good in humanity. I think I've been damaged, though,
because today, I am not sure if still I can say,
yes, these people that have taken
everything
from me besides my breath, are good.

I have been taught that I am a product of God's love
and yet, I have nary an item
for my name to claim. The other men look at me
like I am weak, and maybe I am. 'You gotta play harder,
do *not* give them what they want.'
They have me, though.
They have my family. They have my privacy,

they have my integrity,
hell, they have my name
(a number is not fit for a human being).
What more do I give?
I haven't figured out that bit yet. What even happens when I do?

But, I do it- I play- because I am bored
and I am unhappy
and what will really happen if I lose?

So I'll wait until the moon has devoured the sun
and the sky has turned into pink ash,
for the morning brings another opportunity
to play their game
once again.

This Game Ain't No Game
Daniel "Vito" Johnson

I receive countless letters and hear from many people telling me how my lyrics and thug ways are missed on the streets. I often hear "Vito, you was a real n---a! They don't make 'em like you no more" or "the streets ain't the same without you." While I appreciate the love I find it ironic because I ain't the same Vito no more and the same fame and glamour I was willing to live and die for is the same thing that shames me today.

Like many of you from the hood, I traveled the road in search of a treasure of gold, opened the treasure chest, and found a mirror that revealed a fool. I'm here to tell you today my brothas and sistas, the youth, our future, that this thing they call the game isn't a game at all and it will devour you because you can't even realize how deep into the beast's throat you are. It's a trap, a real deep trap disguised in lies. You see, it never told me that at 19 years of age I would be charged with 5 bodies and placed on death row before I was even found guilty.

To add insult to my pain, the same lyrics and lifestyle I promoted through my music was being used as evidence to slay me. I remember it vividly, sitting in the courtroom, the D.A. playing my videos and songs claiming that I was guilty of murder because I rap about guns. Drugs, the money, the loss/murder of friends, and how before I let someone blast me I'll blast them. In the middle of this nonsense I looked up and realized that I was charged with killing someone who looked just like me and came from the same background as me. The D.A. is trying to kill me for being a product of an environment and unjust system his people created. You see brothas and sistas like me ain't create the hood or the game, we were born into it! At that very moment of realization, when I turned around and looked at both sides of the courtroom and saw the hurt and pain I realized I was played out, tricked and deceived. Our mothers were hurting and this D.A. was smiling.

Reflecting on this and sharing this through writing makes me feel sad for the old me. I see a boy who was lost and became addicted to fame and feeling accepted. I'm not the only one that goes through this ordeal; it is common in our hoods. This is what we ride or die for, to be accepted and respected by our corner and neighborhood. Now listen, don't get me wrong, there ain't nothing wrong with riding for your hood or your team, but what are you/we riding for? If we riding for our hoods then we have to do more than destroy them and terrorize our own community. We ride for power and respect yet how come we can't even make our hoods safe? How many of us are policing our own hoods? We should be the ones our people call on for assistance or help, we should be the ones ensuring that the children, elderly, and women can walk through our territory and not be robbed, harassed, or frightened. I learned that this is what real riders do. I'm writing this as a message to our youth so that we can no longer be fooled or lured by this game whose target is youth of color and especially Black youth. Us! We have to join together whether you like it or not to destroy this Beast of a the prison system that is eating us alive.

I thought long and hard about writing this and one of my biggest fears in this journey and my change was being judged. I lived my entire life being what was expected of me by others. Now I define myself. I write this today not to glorify my past but to warn the younger brothas and sistas about the game; the game is dead. I'm giving it to you raw and uncut, just like my lyrics. I've been through it, had the fame, sold the drugs, rode for my homies and was left behind the lines. One minute I was sharing the stage with Meek Mill; the next I was on center stage in a courtroom fighting for my life. That is how quick this beast can bite you.

I had a voice through hip hop and now I want to use my voice to keep brothas and sistas from falling into the jaws of the Beast. I want to show them the enemy isn't the brothers or sistas up the street from you but rather the system which is responsible for our oppression and conditions of our neighborhoods. The FBI releases statistics every year that show that more white people consume drugs than Black people in the United States, yet why do our neighborhoods suffer the most? Just something to think about.

I know for many my transition is shocking, however, don't get it twisted, I'm still a rider. I still have love for my homies and will never forget ya'll. I just now know what I am riding for. I will never forget the saying that if you want to hide something from a Black person put it in a book. I learned so much, I learned about Elder Russell Maroon Shoats, a former gang leader from West Philly who became a member of the Black Panthers and Black Liberation Army, who is now one of the longest held political prisoners in the world. He has been in prison since 1972. Him and his crew were working to eliminate the oppressive condition in our communities, conditions which created the environment that gave birth to the game I grew up in. His pamphlet "Liberation or Gangsterism" changed my life. If you ever get a chance to read it, read it. (to my people on the outside it can be found online).
So in closing, the only way we can understand our worth is by understanding our history. I was once one of them

brothas that looked at conscious brothas as crazy/shot out, not knowing that this stemmed from a lack of knowledge and understanding of the history and the elements we're up against. Unless we grow up and fight and stand for a cause much bigger than making a name killing our ourselves we will never be remembered for anything of worth and to not be remembered is to never have existed.

Real riders have a duty to fight and pass the torch of struggle to our youth, the same way my Elder Russell Maroon Shoats passed it to me, and the youth like me have a duty to make sure the torch is raised high with a fire that's blazing hot because it's fueled by the hatred and lies that they showed and told us, blazing hot blazing hot because in every state all over the country it's brothas and sistas in cell's who have been tricked and deceived into killing and destroying each other and our hoods. Blazing hot because since the day we were given life the odds have been stacked against us. Blazing hot because this Beast is eating us alive! We have a duty to support one another, and to show real love to one another. Let's keep riding, but riding for a worthy cause - each other! I recommend my brothas and sistas from the hood to enroll in the one Hood United Correspondence Course. We at One Hood United are trying to educate our youth to realize this game is a trap and, most importantly, that we must defend and support our people and neighborhood. Write the address listed below and request to be put on the One Hood United Correspondence Course waiting list.

Book Through Bars ATTn: Address This/One Hood United
4772 Baltimore Ave
Philadelphia, PA 19143

38.7442° N, 90.3053° W
Mikala Rempe

In loving memory of Michael Brown

I wasn't prepared for what this show-me state had
to show me.
I watch my America on the news and don't recognize it
anymore.
We are star-spangled in secrets
An unarmed boy in Missouri yells, "Don't Shoot"
After a fortnight of turmoil, police officers in tanks
scream at camera-men, "Don't Shoot!"
Don't want the world to see
how drunk with power they've become
The way they vomit violence and tear gas into streets,
where little boys play kick the can
while grasping at straws for their life
with the same ten fingers their mother counted
every night before tucking them in.
Michael, did your mother count them one last time
before she tucked you into soil?
Redemption is only found in looted milk from
McDonald's
poured into burning eyes
like manna from somewhere better than here.
College classrooms vanish while a boy in the street
drowns
in his own blood, raped of all its potential,
in this pool that's swim at your own risk,
boy at your own risk,
black at your own risk,
in a pool of we are not here to save you.

He drowns in his story unfolding
faster than the slug that stopped him
and the way America steals boys, because of their skin
and the way it's the color of so many suns going down
too many sons going down.

Dear Society
Christine Hwang

I don't want to die.
Not in pain, not in vain.
But this is the price you say,
the price I pay,
for slaying a life away.

So,
take
take
take away.
For all the ugly things I did yesterday.

Forget about the good I've done,
before the night that I held that gun.
Forget about the person I was,
a son, a brother, a father who loved.

So
strip
strip
strip away,
take it all for your own tomorrow.

Just as took my name and gave me a number,
just as you took my home and gave me a cellar,
rid me of my forgiveness and penance,
and instead, throw me down a death sentence.

So
kill
kill
kill away,

tell them how the monsters pay:

Let good vanquish evil on execution day,
for a villain's blood has been shed away.
Let us rejoice at his death
let true justice ring,
in the face of our justice
in his endless suffering.

The Crowd
Sofia Crutchfield

Political pandering
and hounding for sound bites;
painting a pretty picture
of one-step justice
instead of forging a foundation
I'd want to build a house on.

Holistic solutions are met
with hostile conclusions
by the keep-it-simple crowd,
the crowd that still believes
it costs more money
to house someone for life
than it does to hang them
because that's what makes sense to them
and we all know that gut instinct
is more important than the truth
than the numbers
especially when it comes to matters of life or death.

This is the crowd that doesn't want to think about racism
more than they've already had to, at least
because didn't you make them uncomfortable enough
when you showed them that documentary
in high school
about the slave trade?
About those horrible boats?
Besides, now there's Obama
and Affirmative Action
so what more do you people want from them?

This is the crowd that wants protection.
They'll say it's from thugs
and drive-by's and muggers
but more vital than the protection of their life or money
is protection from the brutal torture
the harrowing guilt
the strenuous brainwork
the cognitive dissonance
of having to change their worldview.

Congressman O'Neill, save us from
challenging ourselves.
Put the people away
like they do at the end of an episode
of NCIS
or Scooby Doo
and then roll the credits
and cut to commercial
because that just makes sense.
Congressman O'Neill, save us from
the confusion
of multi-faceted problems
because we don't like those.
Put the bad men in prison
so *we* can rest in peace.

Alternative Endings
Brian Medich

"Brandon, what is it you want to do with your life?" asked Principal Hurley of the alternative high school in Harlem I went to. I pretended not to hear. I'd already checked out for the day. The bell had rung ages ago. I had done my time, but Hurley had yanked me into his office. A little white old man, screaming in a shrill voice like my mom's, telling me I'd disobeyed school rules. Like I gave a shit.

So what the fat gym guy caught me smoking in the handicap stall. I wasn't hurting nobody. I was just trying to get my nerves down. But this fat guy came in, took me by the shirt, and made me do laps for hours. Sweat dripping, he yelled at me saying, "you'll learn not to do that, boy," as the whole room laughed. He'd be getting his. No one messes with me after today.

Hurley finally let me go, giving me his disappointed look. Then acting surprised when I didn't react, he said, "you're disappointing me, Brandon." Like I'm stupid or something.

I got up, popped a joint in between my teeth and lit it. I turned to look at Hurley and puffed, "damn, and all these time I've been trying so hard." I didn't wait for his reply. My cousin was waiting for me outside and I was on top of the world. I was walking toward the car when I heard that fat pig open his mouth. It was the gym teacher.

"I thought I taught you a lesson today, boy." He smiled so big. I wanted to kill him. Cut his snout off. He came towards me. Entitled. "Put it out," he said, reaching for my mouth. I swatted his hand. His face reddened. He grabbed my shirt and I punched him in the eye. Then he fought back.

I was on the ground now, suffocating from his weight. I couldn't move. His face was inches from mine. The joint was burning my throat. I was losing, bad. I closed my eyes

My eardrums exploded and I tasted blood. I felt no more pain. The gym teacher seemed to be losing his grip, so I pushed up. I opened my eyes and breathed deep. I didn't know how I got him off me. I started touching my face to find the blood. Couldn't find it. The gym teacher wasn't moving. I looked at my cousin who was smiling, laughing almost, "Brandon, I'm so in man. I'm so in. No way I'm not getting in." A pistol was in his hands. He had shot the gym teacher right through the back of the head.

Mr. Hurley's question plays over and over in my mind now. "Brandon, what is it you want to do with your life?" It's all I hear all day. But, if he were actually here, I'd answer him now.

"Mr. Hurley," I'd say, "I want to get out." I'm serving a 10-year sentence.

The Ride In
Jason Russin

Dust surrounds me,
I breathe it in
Through the open windows
As this deathtrap hurtles,
Down this dry desert road.

Chains jingle,
Inmates murmur,
The wheels roll,
The engine roars,
As we hurtle towards hell.

I step off
Greeted with the suns hot kiss,
And a dusty slap to the face,
The dry ground crackles beneath my feet,
I realize,
The ride doesn't end here.

The Things They Carried
Maggie Brennan

When they told me to strip
down I knew it wasn't personal
knew they had to check
that I wasn't going to pull a shiv
outta my ass.
Nothing quite so glamorous
as entering a prison.

Check in.
Hand over your
personhood.

The guy behind the counter
bagged and labeled
the contents of my life.
Everything I thought
was important enough
to carry around.

The picture of Shelly
on her birthday
and the gift card to Starbucks,
little increments of me,
the shiny penny Nan
told me to keep for
good luck.
A business card
so worn and yellowed
I don't know if it was mine
or someone else's.

My wallet.
Cracked shitty leather
stuffed to the brim
with crap.
But it's my crap.
Can't even walk right
with my pockets so empty.

I feel crooked
for the first time.

The Mural
Grace Austin

Prisoners filed through the bright hallway
each wall adorned with upbeat murals freshly touched up
by local community groups
As they walked to their destination, the expressive faces of
the surrealistic men and women of all different ethnicities
transcribed by artists on the cement walls reminded them
that a world outside existed.
Through these murals many men found hope
they saw themselves, they saw their lovers.
The colors danced off their corneas and diverted them
for at least half a second from their impending doom.
As they left the hall, they felt a piece of themselves leaving
too.
What was that feeling?
Why did they only feel it there?
Some inmates petitioned the warden to allow them to
draw their own murals throughout the prison.
"Let us express ourselves" the paper said.
The bleakness of their cells never again let them
underestimate the power of creation.
"No graffiti" said the warden.
"Fine."
They were given brushes
crude paint
and a few walls in the gymnasium
and told not to fuck it up.
The men knew the weight of the responsibility they had
just been handed.
With these paints they could lift spirits
change decisions
maybe even stop suicide, murder, and hate.

An abstract drawing of a woman there
a religious symbol here
a landscape over on the other side
they were building a window into another world
they were building something to hold on to.
Color
is a wonderful distraction.

Doorway to Oblivion
Anne Scherer

Standing
withered and worn
etched lines of time and storms,
embedded in the grain

what dwells beyond holds so much anxiety
takes my breath and runs, racing towards the edge of
oblivion
racing to be away from here, daily
face to face with my fears

Standing
withered and worn
etched lines of time and internal storms,
embedded in my skin.

Contained
Ainsley Bruno

Prison is a state of mind
you cannot contain my thoughts
the way you can contain my body.

My well-being
my health
my dreams
are free to wander
further than the 8x8 foot room
I am trapped in.

You cannot take away my sight,
the way you can take away ability
to grasp
to taste
to feel.
I am still free to imagine
what my senses have been deprived of
while I am trapped.

You cannot put a number on my ambitions
the way you can put a number on me.

My name
my legacy
my case
will last longer
than the guards who lock me in the room
that I am trapped in.

Species x
Lorena Lipe

It would have been easier
to breath through a noose
wrapped tightly around my neck.

It would have been neater
to press my flesh
against the edge of a blade
in front of an audience.

My mother
would not have cried
as hard
had I been strapped
to a chair,
and turned into
a human live wire.

A bullet through my chest
or lethal fumes
forced through my nostrils
would have made me feel
more alive.

Lethal juices
invading the blood
running through my veins
would have had my heart
beating faster.

To know that there are people
out in the free world
who will rejoice

at the news of my death
makes me want to beg
whomever is up there
to speed up this process.
Death is an easy trip to take
when you have been reduced
to a species
that falls somewhere between human
and monster.
Genus: unknown.

Math
Shyla Bergin

When I was in school, I enjoyed math.
Numbers had always been my thing,
Until the number of deaths became too high,
And the price of drugs became too low.
That balance threw me off.
I then started hating numbers,
But worse I started hating myself.
I guess if you hate two things at once,
They can become one.
Today I am a number.
I belong to the state,
They are holding my body in a cell.
Not as a person, but as a number,
A statistic.
I have no place in society,
Because this number is branded on me.
Maybe I can learn to love myself,
But I could never love my number.

The Beat
Jason Russin

Click, clack
click clack
The sound of the guards shoes on the cement floor,
the only sound I hear as I walk to chow.
It is loud, it consumes me
it reminds me everyday where I am.

The loud clanking and locking of prison doors,
the sliding of cell doors and the jangle of guards keys.
All parts of a rhythmic beat that keeps me up at night.

Some days it is classical,
others country, hip hop or rock.
These sounds are a beat,
a beat that is stuck in my head,
a beat that is a part of my being,
a beat that will never leave me
a beat like the one of my heart.

The Dance
Daniella Sklarz

Not your Nutcracker
Similar nonetheless
Dirtied feet like painful toes
Many girls or too many hoes
A special costume for me
It's orange and fitted just right
The guards banging on cells
Like the jingling of Christmas bells?
A cold cell like, like
An air-conditioned theater.
Clapping hands like fornicating friends
Oh the sounds.
A tragic staged death
Except there's real blood here.
Not your Nutcracker.

You Are My Catalyst
Emily Dalgo

You are my catalyst;
A reason.
Something to believe in.
You are my muse;
An addiction.
Something to breathe in.
You are my impetus;
A spectacle inside my cell,
Classified, safe inside,
With me in this hell.

I Know Pain
D'angelo

I know pain like the back of my hand
I've felt it on my skin like wind from a fan
I've cradled it like a baby and rocked it to sleep
Spilled it all over my clothes and all over my sheets
I've loaded it into a gun and forced others to accept it
I harmonized with its voice and drove it in every direction
It walks when I walk and breathes when I breathe
Yeah I know pain and pain knows me
It mimics my behavior and dares me to get mad
It wants me, haunts me and taunts me when I'm glad
It made its way into my life and won't let me be
Yeah I know pain and pain knows me

Pain on Paper
Elijahwon Watts

This is just not a tree
This is just not nature
This is just not a pack of paper
This is my feelings
So why do you say writing doesn't
Show anything
I put my pain on paper
It cools me down
So
I am going to write and read

Dear Anybody
Christine Hwang

Don't leave me here alone,
to wake up and be met
with lost memories and regret
things I left unsaid,
the person I used to be,
the person that was free,
free from this hell,
free from this cell,
free from just me.
Don't leave me here alone,
to get twisted and caught up
in the web of my ugly thoughts,
a battle that I've lost,
hallucinations
condemnations
realizations.
Don't leave me here alone,
alone to suffer the strife
of this miserable, meaningless life,
with nightmares that are mean,
and dreams that can't be seen.
Every day
the same
the same
mundane
game.
Don't leave me here alone,
alone with all my demons,
and nothing good to believe in,
nothing but stress,
stress and duress,

a big fucking mess.
Losing grip of reality,
on the brink of insanity,
anybody
somebody
just not nobody
hear my pleas,
and let me be,
a human being.

Isolation
Anne Scherer

Like a snake, isolation wraps its body tightly around and around
squeezing
suffocating
the air barely breathes.

    Societies imposed constrictions on the hearts of the hurting, the desolate, is a cruel statement of the world that we live in today. And this is Humanity? To cut off

cut down

cut in
two
the lifeless skin dividing the flesh...baring bones.

The skeletal aloneness of the demoralized lies entombed, mummified.

Deprivation
soul starvation

the spirit soars forth and cries, "Oh my God, I long for you!"

The Gargoyle of isolation feeds on the flesh of friendship...family.

And the world grows smaller and
                                    smaller

and very soon there is nowhere and no one to turn to.

Even the self has been destroyed.

The Boa devours
whispering
    (hiss)

"Nobody wants you!"
    (hiss)

Unsociable
Garrett Hubbell

Solitary, shadows scream upon the walls
Alone, seeking a voice to speak to, to hear...
Miserable, madness unleashes dark twisted violence
Pain, grows like a tulip on a day in May
Concealed in a world of not knowing
What time is it? What day is it? Is it morning? Is it night?
Confined in a locked up chest
Ready to be released like a jack in the box, springing up and down
Imprisoned in prison, tormented and traumatized
Sorrow awakens me as a large gasp of air makes my heart thump
Guilt nestles deep inside, hibernating like a bear for winter
Hunger, my rib cage threatens my body and presses out stubbornly
Unattractive bones are illustrated down to every detail
Thoughts running through the mind, I miss my wife, her adoring good looks and her passionate kisses
Aggravations bother the soul, festering like scabs on un-nurtured skin
Time is slipping away, slowly, an hourglass moves quicker
Quiet, the air speaks to me, as I have nobody else to speak to
Murmurs and whispers spew out of my mouth to try to remember to speak
Fear, when will I get out? Will I go crazy?
Solitary, not human nature
Get me out of here
It's a nightmare

Crocus
Alfred "Spoken Truth" Dearing

Another harsh winter, another cycle completed
I'm still struggling, stuck between polarities balanced
A dark shadow hovers; still I'm gone to November
Won't be til early spring before I rise from the rubble
I'm budding, my cries watering
I'm cultivating thoughts of importance
But positivity seems distant in my family
My cousin Iris molested me during my times of metamorphosis
I was robbed blind of my colors
When stimulated my smile be bright yellow, to a frown that's purple
Disciplined by my petals, I produce a sense of purpose
Spraying scent of reproduction, pollen enters
Sending excitement signals to my stamen
Orgasms flow from my pistils
Ovaries contain the purest embryo
Seeds distribute the finest nutrients
I'm Crocus, the flower Vitality
Coasting through the vernal equinoxes
Freedom sings when the birds humming
Bees buzzing therapeutic melodies
Not a word spoken
Germs effective, one grain manifests seeds of tomorrow
Though we bloom from sorrow
I'm Crocus, the flower!
Descending from heaven's garden
To fight circumstance borrowed
Nothing lasts forever
Soon time will fade my petals in the wind like feathers
By then, my legacy will be forever remembered
Stained in the minds of my followers

Reincarnated when germinated, I breathe from the
elements of power
Representing hard conditions, victimized by hard times
But still I rise from the sunshine, beauty defined!
Deep rooted in your smile, I stand
The warmth of your nurturing hands, I'm energized
Like the rose that grew rough from the concrete
I'm bound by my hand and feet
Tossed to the world to roll to pieces
Dead flowers all around me
But I'm back, in the form of Crocus, the flower
Look, how spring strengthens me!

4-12-76 – No Ending

Bloom Grown From a Crack in the Wall
Beverly Jaynes

Reaching light from deceptive darkness,
Its seed mysteriously nurtured within,
Exposing walls cannot contain its growth,
Breaking free unexpectedly,
From bleak, stark surroundings,
The bloom, the more beautiful,
For its unlikely flourishing,
A surprising sign of hope,
A prevailing life force,
Graced by opportunity.

Heat Waves
Jason Russin

The heat blazes,
I lie,
Tossing, turning,
In a pool of sweat.
Here there is no AC,
Here there are no fans.
Only the heat.
I look outside through the bars,
The heat waves dance in the air,
This is not a mirage,
This is real life.

The Weather in Solitary
Brian Medich

The forecast says it's raining
But I can't even shower
Memories of backyard floods
An inmate clogs his toilet.

The forecast talks about the leaves
But I can't see them changing
Memories of raking red debris
An inmate mops another's blood.

The forecast says it's overcast
But I can't tell the difference
Memories of foggy afternoons
An inmate's ceilings always grey.

The forecast says there's thunder
But I can't even hear it
Memories of homemade hideaways
An inmate's banging never stops.

The forecast says to bundle up
But I can't get a blanket
Memories of snowball fights
An inmate throws his shit.

Drown
Marisa Fein

I see the outside world pass by in squares, the image distorted by metal wires that crisscross over the window of the van. I haven't seen freedom in over ten years. It's funny that not much has changed. Resigned to my cell, lying on the cool metal of a rectangle that barely resembles a bed, I would imagine the outside world. I imagined flying cars, robots that would clean rich people's houses, kids running around shooting each other with laser guns like the ones in the old science fiction shows that my dad used to watch. I believed that the outside world must have been changing as the grey walls of my cell stayed the same.

But there aren't any flying cars and the kids run around with cell phones instead of toy lasers and I'm not sure why this frustrates me so much. I look at the clock on the van's dashboard and am reminded that, unless these inventions come about in the next three hours and twenty-four minutes, they are things that I will never see. Another minute goes by.

The van's driver, an old white guy with a grey beard that tickles his chin, begins to hum a tuneless song. I want to kick the back of his seat but there's no point and besides, who would listen to a man who's as good as dead anyways?

That's what the prosecutor had said, the real smug guy who never even bothered to look me in the eyes as he announced to the court that I was "an injustice to society, a danger to your wife and kids. The culprit of murder." The jury members leaned forward in their seats then, their eyes wide, enjoying the show. I swear I saw the hint of a smile cross one of the jurors face, an old woman with leathery skin, as the prosecutor laid out the reparation that the state was seeking: death.

I remember hearing about the guys on death row as a kid, reading about the weekly executions in the paper. And I never questioned it, never thought it was strange that, just two hours north of my home in my quiet Texas town, over three hundred executions had been carried out. But these deaths could be justified by simple logic, people said. An eye for an eye. It all made sense. Hit me and I'll hit you back.

And I always hit back, every time, no matter what. I hit back the time that my brother tried to throw boiling water on me after I got dirt on his shoes. I hit back after the owner of the convenience store on the corner accused me of stealing a candy bar. I hit back even when there was no one left to hit, after my dad left and my mom was beaten by the man that came around three weeks later to take his place. My whole life has been blow after blow, but my reflexes haven't always been fast enough to protect me.

The van turns off of Main Street and onto a deserted, one lane road. The trees are thick here, the sky clear without a cloud in sight, but I wish for rain. I wish for a downpour, an act of God so fierce that it would sweep me up in its clutches and soak me in something, anything, that could cleanse me, clear my vision and restore the part of me that escaped as soon as I first heard the click of steel bars closing.

It's the rain that I miss, the soft touch of a drop of water sliding down my back, tickling the side of my face and squirming into the cracks of my shoes. I miss the sunlight too, especially on days when the light would touch my skin through my barred window, strained through the steel but still present in my cell, nonetheless. But, sometimes, when I would be granted a few rare moments of silence, when I could close my eyes and almost forget that my life had been confined to a metal cage, I could remember what it was like to be engulfed in sunlight. I could never remember what it was like to be drowned in rain.

And I want to drown. I want to soak in my crimes and breathe in the sweet water of the tears of my victims. I want my lungs to fill, to expand and gasp and burn and eventually accept and remember that not all those that breathe can live. I guess in that way, I am already drowning.

Ten minutes have passed. Three hours and fourteen minutes remain.

I could have done it. I could have wrapped my fingers around her neck and squeezed until the skin bruised and the space between my hands grew smaller. I could have kicked her, twice, first in her stomach and then in her head. I could have heard the sound that my boot made as it made contact with her skull, breaking what was once whole into two. They tell me that I did it.
But I swore on my innocence, I cried and pleaded with my lawyer that I hadn't done it, that I was not capable of murder. He had nodded and checked the score of the game on his phone. I didn't even have to ask him what it was, either way I was losing.

The victim's mother had cried in court, her eyes dripping like the rains of a hurricane. I later saw the same tear stained face on the six o'clock news on an old TV as they transferred me to my cell. She had been saying something about me, asking why anyone would commit such a crime, how anyone could be so stupid as to inflict death on another person when they knew that the consequences would, in turn, be the same. The reporter had shoved the microphone out further then, pushing for more from the woman who had just attended the trial concerning her only daughter's murder.

"If he knew they would seek the death penalty," the reporter asked, "then why do you think he did it?" The guards pushed me forward then, one of them digging his overgrown fingernails into my arm through my state-issued jumpsuit. The reporter expected Texas's past relationship with executions to have deterred me from committing the act for which I was accused. But she didn't understand, nor did the judge or the attorney. None of them understood that the crime that was being described, the crime that had resulted in the death of a young woman, was not an act of logic. There is no logic in a face that has been kicked in, in the black and blue marks of a bloated stomach that houses a heart that has stopped beating. They say I did it but I couldn't have. There's no way.

I close my eyes as if I'm going to go to sleep, as if I don't have only three hours and eight minutes before I am forced to sleep forever.

In my dreams, God is on trial and I am the judge. There is no defense or prosecution, no jury. Just me and the big guy, alone in a courtroom. And I open my mouth, my mind filled with images of the gangbangs that happened in the parking lot of my childhood apartment building, of the textbooks at my school that had their covers torn off and had been published before I was even born, of the face of the police officer who had told me that he was sorry, that the knife had punctured my only brothers lung and popped it like a balloon, all because he had been wearing the wrong set of colors in the wrong part of town. But when I open my mouth with the intent of putting these images into words, instead I hear myself scream. I scream like an animal, like a dog that's been left bleeding on the streets, like a little boy who grew up in the projects.

I open my eyes because the car is slowing. My muscles tense until I realize that we've only paused at a stoplight. My eyes meet with the driver's in the rearview mirror. We stare at each other for a minute, a collection of sixty seconds, before he looks away and the light changes and the car begins to move again.

I had known the victim. She was my connection, the one who would knock on my door so late at night that it was closer to dawn than sundown. It had always been strictly business between us. She would step into the living room of my apartment and I would give her the money, all in cash, and she would hand me the bag of pills. And then I would have three of the capsules sliding down my throat before she was even out the door.

But then she hadn't knocked on my door in a while and I was starting to see things that weren't there, started to swear I could hear my brother in the kitchen talking about how this bitch had cheated me, how she was selling to everyone in town but me, how I shouldn't be surprised because I was worthless and living off of welfare checks and was worse than scum, worse than the dirt that got caught in his shoes.

I began to wait, to spend my whole days at home just in case she came by with her latest score. I began to call my other connections only to find that they had all run dry. I began to sleep in front of my door until I stopped sleeping all together and instead spent my nights staring out the peephole and counting the number of people who walked by.

I had gone through my last two cases of beer when she did finally knock. I didn't know if it had been days or weeks or even years since I had last seen her but either way I could swear that the world had changed since our last encounter, that there had been revolutions and uprisings and wars that had all been fought while I had waited for the sound of her knuckles to echo through my apartment.

I invited her in. She apologized, said something about her supplier disappearing on her, about this being the last of what she had. I told her that it didn't matter, I would take it anyway, that the supply that she gave me could usually keep me satisfied for at least a week, longer if I paced myself. And then she hesitated before pulling out the bag, the bag that contained half as many pills as it should have, and then I felt nothing, not angry or sad or even excited about my high that she held in her hand.

And then I was sitting at a table in a room that had one light and a man in a suit was yelling, telling me to admit that she had broken things off between us and that I had gotten angry and killed her. I told him the truth, that I didn't know what he was talking about. I didn't mention that the last thing I remembered was seeing my brother and him taking my hand and squeezing it tight, crying even though I had never seen him cry before. And I remembered not being able to tell if there was blood under his fingernails or if it was all in my imagination.

But I can't think of this now, I can't think of my brother or the victim or how her mother had buried her face in her hands and how her body had shaken after the jury had announced their verdict. The driver fiddles with the radio. He pauses at a country station before turning it off entirely. I try my hardest not to look, not to notice that I only have two hours and fifty-two minutes left.

I heard stories while in my cell, heard whispers from the other inmates about how there is nothing clean about executions, about how one time the execution team couldn't find a suitable vein and spent forty-five minutes poking the inmate like a pincushion.

I stare out the window, at the blur of trees that we pass, and think about death. I think about the chemicals that will spread through my veins, making their way to my heart, slowing my breath in the process. I think about how my eyes will become so heavy that they are forced to close, my last image of the world being of cinderblock walls and men with somber faces, of my reflection in the glass paneling, of me being strapped down to a gurney with the taste of my last statement still on my lips. And I wonder if I will think about the victim and speculate if this too is how she passed, under circumstances that come with a life being cut short. I think about whether in those last moments I will think of spaceships or metal bars or the sound that rain makes on tin roofs until I can no longer think of anything other than a blackness that I won't be able to tell is from the back of my eyelids or something else entirely. And I think about if I had done it, if I could claim the victim as my own, if I would see any justice in my execution.

I try to glance at the dashboard clock but the driver's hand is in the way. But it doesn't matter because I know that the clock is still ticking and that I shouldn't be upset about this because this is what justice looks like, like a twenty-seven year old man handcuffed in the back of a white van traveling at forty-three miles an hour on the way to an execution that the court has deemed just and fair. Justice sits next to me, on the fabric of the neighboring seat and whispers in my ear.

You could have done it.

Cherry Red
John Raley

There's never been so much blood on the floor
With the clanging, the banging of my cellmate's door.
A shattering sound breaks the silence of night,
The initial roar of a crowd expecting a fight.

Red on red hues stain the tile.
The cuts from the knife got the tissues, spared the bile.
Help to stop it was lame at the time,
Heads turned sideways then downward on a dime.

I felt helpless as he cried against the brick,
Not knowing if I was next to take the hit.
There's no place to run when your cell is packed,
And the guard starts to smile but then turns his back.

From light to dark, the puddle's near my bed.
It seems so dreamlike, a beautiful cherry red.
A painting well matted will frame this memory
Of a cherry red flow across a jailhouse floor.

Drunks: Losers
Rick Lyon

Not a complete loser, not dead yet,
he held a job, briefly, at a car dealership,
quit, complaining of poor health, gout,
compounded by drinking he tried to hide.
But how hide a volatile child-man
in a lumbering three-hundred pound body,
fearful, all but drained of self-respect,
when your ex-wife wishes you were dead
and your children want nothing to do with you?
For two seasons, he played professional football
and claimed he was a fighter, worth something to someone.
He'd found a gullible woman to pay his way, assuage his wounds,
but she'd buckled likewise under the strain.
No surprise, when the police arrive one morning
to quell a domestic dispute, death threats,
self-hatred directed anywhere but at oneself.
And now he lies in a hospital room, pulled back from the brink,
where the sheriff has served a restraining order
and he may enter a month-long treatment program,
not exactly a loser, not yet, not dead.

Audacity
G. Leaks

I have the AUDACITY to keep going with relentless optimism and tenacity,
even though it seems that adversity never tires with harassing me...
Questions they asking me, is equivalent to blasphemy,
for I've been created, in the image of thou creator
Thou shalt never bow down to the feet of thou oppressors;
Nor respect favorable result confessors
or any weak spirit, whom-wait-for-the-lord(s)-to-bless-it...
I have the AUDACITY to display strength,
received nourishment from the bosom of my mother;
The days and nights I suffered from hunger pangs, only made me tougher,
Now I cant get enough of... PAIN!
Which leads to the gain... of strengthening my spirit and mind frame...
RAIN; which will eventually lead to sunshine,
birds, bees and butterflies, the smell of new life in the air
...the smell of inner-peace...
I have the AUDACITY to plant a seed,
and closely monitor the development of it's fruition,
so I can properly nourish the minds of our future, with my harvest...
I have the AUDACITY to honor our future,
for they are the inheritors, who shall inherit us;
For they are the inheritors, who shall inherit the chaos that we've created...
I have the AUDACITY to repent;
Hell bound, even though I'm heaven sent
my long walk towards the light of liberation is evident;

What? Y'all thought y'all was free, because America got a president?...
That look like us? Can he cook like us? Read and decipher a book like us?
endure all the bullshit we took... LIKE US?
POWER to the people? What POWER is that supposed to be? BLACK? HOW?
When you won't even take the initiative to take care of your child
No parental guidance, so they run wild
While you perpetrate for the crowd
Talking non-sense extremely loud
Ignorant and proud...
If you would just take a second to shut the F#@K UP and listen, then you shall receive knowledge
from a brother who's polished,
whose never spent a nanosecond in college
My STRUGGLE is Harvard... My CELL is Yale;
As I blaze this trail, I have no intention to fail
I shall succeed, in my journey towards reaching GREATNESS...
I HAVE THE AUDACITY TO BELIEVE...

No More Innocence
DJ

Innocence lost, long, long ago
Before even able to crawl, I walked down that road
Life is a game that can't be beaten
Innocence lost for more than one reason
Soul got crushed, spirit got broken
Wide awake, but still feel like I'm sleepin'
Rotten mouth, but voice so sweet
The game is easy, but still I cheat
I've cried long as rivers, lakes and creeks
I once was innocent, a time not known
Lost and alone, slowly I've grown
The route I've chosen was wrong
But I found the right way home
I've sinned, I've repented, but innocence still lost
No more innocence!

Realizations
Ainsley Bruno

The crimes I commit
do not
define the person I am outside these walls.
My favorite color
does not
change from yellow to grey because that's all I see.
The world outside
does not
stop turning because I am standing still.

Phone Calls
Aiden Banks

before the series of events

leading to my incarceration
  i was never one much

for talking on the phone
one
 word
    responses

perhaps a place

perhaps a time

   that was then

   this   isn't   then

failure to abide

by what they deem

   acceptable conduct
has left me stripped
  of what they call
     "privileges"

one
by
one

i regain them

today is my first contact
with her
since god
    knows
        when

21 cents a minute
collect call

far more than my time
in this place
is valued

ring #1

i know exactly the words
to say

ring #3

after all,
how could i not
this conversation
to be

has played over
inside my head
for days
on end

ring #6
every possible question
and comment,

and a response

there could only be
so many

my thoughts are rudely interrupted
by the recording of a man

informing me she can't make it
to the phone

that no,

she will not be accepting a collect call from Clinton
Correctional Facility

i just want to hear her voice

the voice
that i am having
a harder

and harder
time remembering

Depression Is Loneliness Always
Emily Dalgo

Depression is loneliness always
Depression is hunger and thirst that isn't satisfied with
food or drink
Depression is tired
It is endless hours of sleep
That leave me more exhausted
Depression is darkness
It is absent-minded tears
It is shivering under warm covers
It is the dreams that feel like home
But waking up in a place without feeling
Depression is self-conscious
It is afraid
It is fear
Of failure, of friends, of confrontation
Depression makes forced smiles tremble
And throats close.
It takes away words and replaces them with sighs

Where the Forgotten Wait
Maggie Brennan

When they come to visit
I know
I know that they have secrets
and jokes and afternoon reruns
hanging in the air
between them.

I know they've forgotten.

She twists the ring on her left hand
like she can't quite remember
where it came from.
I do.
I've thought a lot about that day,
about every day.
Confinement does that-
lays it out like those pills in the Matrix-
either think a lot
or not at all.

My baby girl's stretched out
like beachside taffy-
forearms ending
in bony points.
No longer covered by
bouncing infant padding.

We talk a lot.
We say nothing.

Who knew absence ached from both sides?
Or, at least, it aches on mine.

Because I know
they've forgotten.
They've forgotten me.

I wave, because we're not allowed
to hug.
I think those elbows might have cut
me anyway.
I say that, and she huffs a smile
that's trying too hard.

They leave.
I stay.

Another Love Song
Michael Drummond

Niah girl, Niah girl, you are my whole world
I wish I was at home with you to give you diamonds & pearls
I'm coming home very soon, I hope you wait for me
And sometimes when I sleep at night I see you in my dreams
You make me smile, you make me frown
Girl I hate them ups & downs
And as I'm in this cell right now
My head keep spinnin' round & round
With thoughts of you & thoughts of me
Like do she still have love for me
Like would she ever take me back
All I can do is wait & see
'Cause when I come home, Imma try my hand
Even if you gotta man
I know you said we would just be friends
But baby, all I need is one more chance
To earn your heart
And keep your heart
Never ever leave you heart
My love for you will never stop
Unless you take & break my heart
Then at that point I have no point
For life
I hope you get my point
'Cause at this point I end my song
You can even call it a poem
But baby I'm really, really sorry if I did you wrong
And this is just another love song

Stranger
Ian Luciano

My little princess
You are still so young
Too innocent to understand
The mistakes that Daddy has made
I hope you read this one day
When you are ready
And know that I would take it all back
Baby girl
To see you now, just once

These grey walls are my canvas, blank and open to interpretation
I stare at them
Picturing your face
Do you have your mother's eyes, or mine?
Did you get daddy's big ears, or mommy's bright smile?
What is your name?
These questions, lingering in my mind
Unanswered, the mystery that steals my sleep
Do you think about me?
Wonder where I am?
What I am doing?
What I have done?

I fantasize
Of the moments I have missed
Have you spoken your first word?
Have you left your mother's warm cradle?
Made use of your soft, tender feet
I imagine the radiant glow on your face
As you stumble across the carpet, back to mommy's loving embrace

I wait
Not for the day that I am free
But for the day I find you
Memorize your face
The day I fall asleep
To the sound of your soft voice in my head
I pray
Every night my love
All I desire
Is to one day say your name in my prayers

Her Eyes
Vlada Grayton

I can see it in her eyes,
The pain she feels.
The sadness that comes upon her.
The happiness that goes through her when she sees me
The despair and shame she feels.
Knowing that the women that gave birth to her
Killed a man.
But I had every right to hurt this man.
What would you do if someone touched your child like that?
Would you walk away from it?
Ignore it?
Pretend it never happened?
NO.
You would do anything in your power to hurt that person,
Twice as hard as they hurt you.
I do not regret what I did.
All I regret is not being able to be with my daughter
Each and every day.
Watching her grow up
Go to her first day of school
Have her make friends
Go on play dates.
I will not be there for all of that.
The only time I have with her
Is when she comes to visit me.
In this hellhole you call a prison.
The place that sucks out all your freedom.
The place that I will spend half of my life in.

Ghost Dad
Juan

Here one day and gone the next
Where did he go? My little voice vexed
Growing up without a dad, that I did
So I grew up a fatherless kid
Every three years he would call me
And every three years he told the same lie
He said he was going to pick me up
But he never did, so I guess he ain't even care
Only time he called was when he got locked up
I was always happy to talk to him, it felt like good luck
When he finally came to see me
I thought I was dreaming
Wow! I finally saw my dad
My feelings were no longer bad
A spitting image of him, that's what I looked like
When I saw his face, I couldn't believe my sight
As soon as I closed my eyes, he was gone from the light
I could no longer see him, I tried with all my might
Here one minute and gone the next
Where did he go? My little voice vexed
My dad, he left me, he left me alone
So I said forget him
I'll learn to be grown on my own

One Decision, Ten Seconds
Jen Holthaus

One decision, ten seconds
Take the car and drive
Feel your pocket, just in case
Your bullet backup plan

Four cops, sirens now
Plans are crashing down
Feel your pocket, just in case
There is no backup now

Sixteen years, four months
Hardly even lived
Feel your pocket, just in case
You'll never need it now

Twenty bars, two mates
What if he has a gun?
Feel your pocket, just in case
You are far too young

Six school dances, four best friends
They'll never understand
Feel your pocket, just in case
Why did you have a gun?

Eighteenth birthday, still here you are
Mother comes to see
Feels her pocket, just in case
No birthday card for you

Ten years later, life's gone on
No one stopped to wait
Feel your pocket, just in case
You've lost all that you've had

Knocked Up
Vlada Grayton

      Eight months,
Three weeks
      Three hours.
That's how long I have been in prison for.
      Eight months,
Two weeks,
      Three hours
Is how long I have been pregnant for.
No healthy food
      No love and affection
  No family or friends.
Nothing that can make me happy again.
No freedom
      No chocolate
No sunshine and smiles
Just a cold white wall keeping me away from the world.
No privacy
      No husband
  No cell phone
Just me and my baby, who I am ready to meet.
No name
No knowledge of the baby's sex
No baby clothes
I can still feel the kicks against my stomach.
  No morning sickness
No period
No food temptations
Just the deep, hard love I have for my unborn baby.
Four weeks
  Two days
      Three hours.

Till I can finally hold my baby close to me for the last time

The Duty of Leaving Imprints
Anthony Winn

The only time for shoes are in church
praying with old souls
who danced to the heartbeat
of a drum till the sun rose
balanced a calabash on their head-wraps
walking down dirt roads
bare feet with no soles

sit down, let me tell you a story feet

Honor those who took flight
tip-toed between the moonlight
blistered, hard to catch
Harriet Tubman feet
getaway, store away
I remember Nigger Foot, Hanover Va.
the severed reek of strange fruit

overripe-go-hard-against-the-grain-feet

Walk with the immortal footsteps
of Irene Morgan grandstanding on Jim Crow
who stood firm on hostile grounds
never lay down, no days off
what is a vacation feet
flat-footed, tripled their worth
can we Xerox Ms. Ursula Burns

coming up on the rough side of the mountain feet

I've known feet that marched alone
to chase and secure dreams

trailblazing
with a delicate sense of urgency
so others could follow
help you find your way
unselfish as Leymah Gbowee feet

one before the other, we stand on our own

A Way Out
Tatiana Shanique Laing

Ralph was that young guy that you had to notice. He had a smile so bright it'd put the sun to shame. A handsome young fella, a tall lean boy. I mean, you knew for sure he was trouble. He sagged his pants and wore a sharpie tattoo of a teardrop near his right eye- he was too much of a punk to betray his bible-beating mother by actually getting inked. But there was a glimmer in his eye when he raised his hand in calculus to answer a question no one else knew. He swore he was only in the class because his mama made him take it. But his absences and failure to complete any homework assignments didn't fool me. It's this type of thug that was the most dangerous of all; caught between the ways of the street and his academic talent. These guys just never completely fit in. They ace their exams, but can't be accepted by the top percentile of students due to their reckless behavior. After hours when they roamed the streets in the shadows, they get the worst dares, they have to prove that they aren't more concerned with their books than their brothers.

High-rises cast a black shadow on the already dark nights downtown. The moon struggles to light the air, thick with smog and overcast. Ideal conditions for drug dealing, gang banging and the mischief of boys with time on their hands and something to prove. Loyalty, brotherhood, bravery— terms otherwise positive—motivate unspeakable acts. The dares get more dangerous as the boys get older and the city becomes as familiar as the back of their hands. They know every ditch, and alley, and place to hide when the shit hits the fan. Like soldiers in guerilla warfare, they find their targets and easily obliterate their goals. The boys with the most to prove, the ones who had a future outside of the projects, were the ones who had it the worst. These boys were at the mercy of the night and their older, more cynical brothers.

Ralph, he was one of the good ones. With the grades he had, he could have gotten into Rutgers. But he spent his nights on the streets, after his mama fell asleep. That poor woman thought for sure her boy was the church-going A-student she had raised. And he was, but these damn projects had it out for a good soul like his. It all came down to one night. It was his turn to prove himself. His brothers scurried into an alley to watch him hold up a corner store. If he chickened out, they probably would have beaten the crap out of him. He didn't chicken out. In fact, he walked in confidently waving the gun his brother had handed him, screaming at the cashier to surrender the money. He was brave, he was prideful, but his intelligence didn't quite extend to the ways of the streets. A woman in the store dialed 911 within seconds of Ralph's dramatic entrance. He lived in a small town. The cashier was a deacon at the church he and his mama went to every Sunday. It was too late to cover his face, and too late to run. The police pulled up to the store in droves. His brothers sneaked away from the scene before Ralph could even think to seek their aid.

We all know how this story ends. Unruly black boy tries to rob a store, and an army of white police officers show up. They didn't ask him to explain himself. They didn't allow him the option of surrender. Through the window they saw him pointing the gun at the cashier. That was all the signal they needed to open fire. Ralph didn't have a chance to explain that he never shot a gun in his life, or that he would never shoot the deacon of his own church. He was bewildered and confused. His so-called brotherhood had abandoned him, until the closed casket funeral. They showed up in a group, wearing all black suits and sneakers. How dare they sit in front of me, when they were the reason he was dead. Half of them were my students as well. I know we teachers are supposed to be objective, but I knew Ralph was special. I mean, I thought he was.

After a few weeks of having him in class, I saw that despite his bad behavior, he was doing well on exams. He reminded me of my high school days. He was smarter than I was, effortlessly. I studied late at night and early into the mornings, only to get B's on my exams. I grew up in these same projects. I know what it's like, I know the pressures of this city. I didn't want to end up in a coffin with my mother crying over me like so many of my peers did. So I chose to stay out of trouble, and make something of myself. I stayed in Camden for college because I couldn't afford to go anywhere else and my grades weren't high enough for scholarships. But I made the most of my education and became a teacher here. I wanted to find a nice suburb to move to, but teachers don't get paid enough for all that. But Ralph? He could have been real special. He could have even left the projects altogether with those grades. In him, I saw everything that I once aspired to be. But I ignored the fact that Ralph didn't value his education enough to apply himself, and that no matter how fond I was of him, he refused to show me respect. I ignored the fact that maybe he had no intention of leaving this place. When I was a kid, I wanted success, but I wasn't able to get out of this black hole we so affectionately call "the hood." It drains your hopes and aspirations out of you to the point where you make up excuses in your head for a wanna be thug who messed around and got himself killed. You make up excuses because his unrecognized potential could have granted him a way out. A way out that you never had. I suppose Ralph did find his way out—the way I'll find some day hopefully far in the future.

Forgive Me
DJ

Please forgive me, I promise I will change
Please forgive me, I want to start over again
Please forgive me, I swear Imma make u proud
Please forgive me, I'm sorry and I'll say it loud
Please forgive me, I know I have done wrong
Please forgive me, I just wanna move on
Please forgive me, I'm on my knees and I'm begging
Please forgive me, my angels are crying and my demons are laughing
Please forgive my stupid mistakes
Please forgive the choices I make
Please forgive the lies I've told
Please forgive the secrets I hold
Please forgive the way I think
Please forgive every step I took
I don't want to be labeled as a criminal or crook
I write long stories and read short books
I have a beating heart and sore looks
Please forgive me!!!!!
.

Second Chances Aren't Given, They're Earned
Rufus Avery

Everyday I looked in the mirror and asked myself, "when am I going to get a second chance?" only to let out a long sigh and reply, "I don't know!" Life in prison helped me mature pretty fast and I'm not lying. I came in as a twenty-two year old kid with an I-don't-give-a-fuck-attitude. Thirty years later, I have slowly become a man with dreams to become something other than a statistic.

Over the years I've seen people come and go, and out of the ones that left, a majority of them came right back behind these walls or gates or whatever you want to call it. Pain fills my heart as I pray and hope the laws change for inmates or convicts that are actually rehabilitating themselves because there is no correction about correctional institutions. Staff doesn't give a damn about us! They want us to fail and it's a shame! Counselors and Case Managers don't help because they don't take their job seriously. To them, it's just a paycheck, but to me, it's our lives that are being played with. Walk with me and see what I see...

"Reid, I have a problem!" I stated as I closed Reid's office door behind me, giving us some privacy from the other hundred and thirty or so inmates.

"What's up?" Counselor Reid replied agitated.

"Well," I hesitated before continuing. "I have been incarcerated a little over thirty years now and I am only getting fifteen days halfway house. In the Second Chance Act, it states a year halfway house can be recommended for those incarcerated over a certain period of time. Being that I've never caught a shot or been in any trouble in the last twenty years, I should be eligible for it!"

Reid looked at me with a smirk plastered across his face and chuckled. I already knew his answer by his body language and his demeanor. Here I was, just another black face wanting a second chance to right my wrongs and all I was about to get was another reason why I wasn't going to make it.

"Mr. Gibbons!" Reid stated before clearing his throat. "We could recommend you for a year halfway house but me personally, I don't think that you've changed. You committed several armed robberies within an eight month time span. Not to mention an attempted murder charge you plead guilty too. Me not thinking you've changed is my opinion and you can write it up if you want because I am not going to help you. Now, if you'll excuse me, I have real business to attend too."

I wanted to punch Reid dead in his mouth, then once he was on the ground, stomp the shit out of him. Instead, I didn't let my emotions get the best of me. I held my tongue and exited his office without saying a word. The old me would have snapped but the new me had things in line that had to be taken care of. What would my woman, Nikee, have to say if she found out I wouldn't be home for another five years because I assaulted a staff member? A question I kept in my head ever time I wanted to cause bodily harm to someone. I've been down too long to slip up now and nothing is going to stop me from going home.

Reid's words played over and over again in my head. The man didn't know me at all! Yeah I robbed fifty something businesses in an eight month time span, caught an attempted murder charge and did my time for it. It seems as though that no matter how much you change, everybody will always judge you by your past, always!

CO Macklin broke me out of my thoughts when she called my name and told me I had a visitor. Luckily, I was already prepared to hit the dance floor as we called it when someone comes to see us. I made my way the V-hall and went through the usual strip search before seeing my contact. The feeling of someone coming to see me was a bit of fresh air. It was a place where AI could smile instead of always being on point. That was my momentary freedom inside this hell.

"Hey Boo!" I greeted as I hugged and tongue kissed Nikee briefly before taking my seat.

"How are you baby?" Nikee asked concerned.

"I'm good!" I answered a little bit edgy. "I just can't wait to get the fuck up outta here!"

"Don't worry about it hon', you're not almost home!" Nikee reassured me.

"Nikee, it's just that they aren't trying to give me six months to a year halfway house!" I explained. "They don't see me as the new me, all they see is my past actions and it's driving me crazy."

"Damn what they think!" Nikee stated as tears started to well up in her eyes. "You are a smart and good man. Yeah, you made a mistake, but we all have made mistakes. That one mistake made you a better and more mature man."

All I could do was put my head down so I wouldn't see the tears fall from Nikee's face. She was right and her words put me at ease. The remainder of the visit was nothing but smiles and laughter once we put the situation behind us. Time flew as we ended our visit with a kiss and a hug before leaving. While Nikee was driving home, I was heading for a strip search. After the strip search was done, I got dress and headed back to my unit to lie down. It only took a moment for my mind to wander to the streets as I laid on my back and looked at the ceiling. I thought about what all I missed and what I was going to miss if I didn't stand up for what I believed in. So, I decided to write a speech as to why I deserved a second chance, why I deserved to get more than fifteen days halfway house and to show how I had rehabilitated myself. It was a long shot, but it was worth a shot.

One Month later...

I stood in front of my Case manager, Unit manager, and Counselor with a stern look on my face as I read my speech...

"I, Keith Gibbons, am a federal inmate at USP Atlanta, serving a prison term of four hundred and twenty months for armed robbery and attempted murder. I come before you as an individual who now understands what it means to be responsible for my reckless or negligent behavior. I have taken on a very different approach to leadership. I have taken sound advice by showing younger inmates how to be responsible for their own actions by showing them how to apply positive things in their lives and applying education and knowledge of drug abuse, alcohol abuse, and how that affects our way of thinking and our way of behaving.

Alcohol, drugs and poor education are ninety percent of why our prison system is overcrowding. These are the sources that drive young men and women to the criminal behavior that puts them in these situations, along with bad decisions. That is why I learned how to suppress my negative way of thinking by educating and rehabilitating myself. This is a forever process and I have learned how to apply my talent to things such as writing movie scripts, novels, poetry collections, songs, and children's literature.

I express these achievements not to mislead you in my progress but only to ask that you know the man that I've grown to become in these last thirty years. I ask that you understand that the society that I stole from are losing in a more drastic way. They are losing our youths through gangs, gun violence, drug abuse, and the list goes on. I, as a father, son, and brother now understand responsibility. I have come full circle in the definition of a responsible man."

Tears rolled down my Case Manager's face and I could tell the words I had spoken touched their souls, but I wasn't finished and I continued reading...

"I ask that you review my last thirty years of incarceration and at my request give me six months to a year halfway house, so I can be given the chance to help guide the youths and steer them in the right direction to keep them from going in the direction that got me here. Also, I would like the chance to show the world that I have changed. I ask this request so I can continue to work with young people out in the society that I'm about to return to. I want to share my story with the youth who are on the wrong track heading towards prison or early deaths.

I ask for the opportunity for my request to be taken into consideration. Maybe, just maybe, I will be able to be home to make amends with my family, my community and the society that I once plagued for so long. I know that I can make some significant changes in some young person's life. If not but one life, I would be grateful for that and give them all the knowledge of the outcome of what bad choices can lead to. I want that to be something I can say I left behind, not just the ugliness of my past criminal lifestyle, but the use of alcohol, drug abuse and bad choices.

I thank you for allowing me to pursue this request and I ask that you take all I have presented into consideration."

"Mr. Gibbons, is that it?" Counselor Reid asked as he took off his glasses.

"I learned second chances aren't given, they are earned!" I stated counselor Reid dead in the eyes.

I walked out after I made my last statement and left what I read to them behind. Would I get that second chance or did I waste my time? I didn't know the answer as I returned to my cell and sat on my bunk. I bowed my head in prayer. All I could do was wait, especially since time was all I had anyway. I just hoped that what I had said got through to them.

Seven Months Later...

I guess I didn't waste my time after all. They called me back to the office and let me know that they were putting me in for six months halfway house. After my brief stay at the halfway house, I was home with my wife Nikee, whom I married right after I got out. I still write and I go around to schools and juvenile facilities and mentor the youths. I mainly talk to them about making bad decisions and how it could hinder their futures. After all, I have seen and been through it, and I wouldn't want to change any of it. But I did learn that second chances aren't given, they are earned!

Still Walking... Mile #1*
G. Leaks

"Stopping is not an option for the successful, they keep going with tenacity and relentless optimism until they succeed. If they fall down nine times they get up ten times. Their faith never wanes from failure. They know that each failure brings them closer to the obtainment of victory. The darkness doesn't discourage them, because they know that light is inevitable for those who persevere..."

-Opio

In the depths of my soul, there's a flame within me that's yearning to be ignited.
Searching for the fuel, which will release this flame from captivity,
I've embarked upon a journey, which shall lead me to liberation.
On this path towards GREATNESS, i embrace the trials and tribulations
that's constantly attempting to hinder my progress.
For with each step i take, i gain an immense amount of strength within my being.
Strength from the adversity that i face on a consistent basis;
As well as from the fuel i've inherited from the great spirits
who've embarked upon this path before my existence.
Who've stood unwavering before the hideous face of oppression, with courage and determination.
Determination not to submit or cower in the presence of adversity...

On this long walk towards freedom, it's imperative that i embrace evolution.
Though i yearn to be released from the clutches of physical confinement;
It's the enslavement of the mind, that must be abolished before i can truly appreciate freedom... and consider myself FREE.
THE COMPLETION OF MILE #1.

*This work was inspired from the autobiography of the late great Nelson Mandela's "LONG WALK TO FREEDOM" and I dedicate this to the "STRUGGLE"
KEEP WALKING!

Last Rites Primeval[1]
Robert Johnson

To give this man/male
(a hand to hold)
To hear ye old mother
(speak words of comfort)
To pull, to flow
(to move with life)
 to spit
(a rudimentary blessing)
in fire
(a rudimentary tool)
That I, we, not
(be)
bark, worm
(now)
black ashes
(ever)

---

[1] Poems inspired by "ultraconserved" words found in linguistic research. Ultraconserved words are "a set of such highly conserved words among seven language families of Eurasia postulated to form a linguistic superfamily that evolved from a common ancestor around 15,000 years ago." See "Ultraconserved words point to deep language ancestry across Eurasia." Pagel et al., Proceedings of the National Academy of Sciences of the United States of America, vol 110 no. 21, Mark Pagel, 8471-8476, doi: 10.1073/pnas.1218726110

About the Editors

ALEXA MARIE KELLY (Editor-in-Chief) is grateful for the opportunity to work on Tacenda Literary Magazine 2015. She believes in the power of creative writing to remind us that we are human. Her goal in editing this year's Tacenda was to engage diverse authors from every corner of humanity. Kelly works as BleakHouse Publishing's Chief Editorial Officer, affectionately managing submissions. She would like to thank Professor Johnson and her coffeemaker, without whom this publication would not have been possible.

ROBERT JOHNSON (Consulting Editor & Author) is a Professor of Justice, Law and Criminology at American University, Editor and Publisher of BleakHouse Publishing, and a widely published and award winning author of books and articles on crime and punishment, including works of social science, law, and fiction. He has testified or testified expert affidavits on capital and other criminal cases in many venues, including U.S. state and federal courts, the U.S. Congress, and the European Commission of Human Rights. He is best known for his book, Death Work: A Study of the Modern Execution Process, which won the Outstanding Book Award of the Academy of Criminal Justice Sciences. Johnson is a Distinguished Alumnus of the Nelson A. Rockefeller College of Public Affairs and Policy, University at Albany, State University of New York.

BRIAN MEDICH (Editor & Author) is currently a junior at American University majoring in Political Science and Communication, Legal Institutions, Economics, and Government. He is also minoring in Creative Writing. His dream is to one day be a political lawyer, as well as a novelist. Originally from New Jersey, Brian is the third of four boys. Since coming to AU, Brian has become a member of Lambda Chi Alpha, and is also a Senator in the Student Government. In his free time, Brian likes to hang out with family and friends, write, read, sing, and watch movies.

SOFIA CRUTCHFIELD (Editor & Author) is an American University student majoring in Law & Society and minoring in International Studies. Through coursework and community service, she has seen first-hand the empowering effects of creative writing in the world of criminal justice, and couldn't be happier to support Tacenda Literary Magazine.

ABOUT THE AUTHORS

GRACE AUSTIN is an undergraduate student in the Honors Program at American University. She is a member of the AU women's rugby team and the SPA Leadership Program. She is a Justice and Law major with an interest in Psychology and Behavioral Neuroscience. She became engaged in creative writing when she took Professor Johnson's Deprivation of Liberty Class, and she is very excited to be working with BleakHouse Publishing.

RUFUS AVERY (No bio provided)

AIDEN BANKS is a student at New England College majoring in Criminal Justice.

SHYLA BERGIN was born and raised in Northern Vermont. She studies business at New England College in Henniker, New Hampshire. She loves her family and friends and does not know where she would be without her identical twin sister Miranda.

MAGGIE BRENNAN is originally from Doylestown, Pennsylvania on the northeast side of Philadelphia, but is currently studying abroad at the London School of Economics. Maggie is a junior at American University in Washington, D.C., and she is majoring in Business Administration with a specialization in Management, but she also hopes to add a minor in Creative Writing to her studies.

AINSLEY BRUNO (No bio provided)

EMILY DALGO is an undergraduate Honors student at American University pursuing a degree in International Studies with a focus in Human Rights. Her academic interests range from women's empowerment to environmental protection to prison reform, though all stem from a passion for activism. Dalgo is President of the slam poetry team at AU and continues to write and perform poetry both on campus and in Washington, DC. Dalgo has enjoyed working with BleakHouse to help give a voice to social justice.

D'ANGELO is 20 years old and is currently incarcerated. He is quiet and keeps to himself, but loves to write poetry and learn new things.

ALFRED DEARING is a 36-year-old Free Minds Book Club and Writing Working member. He is currently serving a 24-year sentence in the state of Virginia. As a youth, Alfred was a major contender in amateur boxing. He is a gifted writer and is producing a book of poems written under the pen name "Spoken Truth." He dreams of helping others.

DJ is a 17 year old Free Minds Book Club and Writing Workshop member. He loves to write poetry and rap. DJ's goal is to become a journalist.

MICHAEL DRUMMOND is an 18-year-old Free Minds Book Club and Writing Workshop member. He is currently incarcerated in North Carolina. He loves to read write, sing and rap. Michael dreams of being able to have a positive impact on young lives when he come home.

MARISA FEIN is an undergraduate student at American University pursuing a degree in literature and women's studies. Through her academic pursuits she has developed a passion for women's rights and has worked to further women's empowerment by leading community education events and interning with the DC branch of the National Organization for Women. Through her work at BleakHouse, she has furthered her interest in prison reform and has become an advocate for social justice.

VLADA GRAYTON is a sophomore business major at New England College. She was born in Russia, but moved to Massachusetts in 2001. She has always had a passion for writing stories but was truly able to express herself in Professor Susan Nagelsen's class.

JEN HOLTHAUS graduated from the School of Public Affairs in 2014. She is currently working as a Litigation Paralegal at the law firm of Hughes Hubbard & Reed LLP in Washington, DC. In her spare time she enjoys reading mysteries, exploring DC neighborhoods, and trying new restaurants and cuisines.

GARRETT HUBBELL is currently a senior at New England College in Henniker, New Hampshire. He is originally from White Plains, New York. He majors in Criminal Justice and minoring in Psychology. Hubbell's goals are to become a police officer or corrections officer.

CHRISTINE HWANG is a senior in the honors program at American University majoring in Justice and Law with a minor in Psychology. Hwang maintains a deep interest in prison reform and social justice advocacy. Her current advocacy work involves drawing attention to errors and unfairness in death penalty cases. Hwang ultimately hopes to pursue law school and a career in capital litigation.

BEVERLY JAYNES (No bio provided)

DANIEL "VITO" JOHNSON was raised in North Philadelphia, Pennsylvania. He's been through some challenging times. He believes his trials and tribulations made him the man he is today. He strives every day to become an example for troubled youth: To teach them to be different, to strive for greatness, and to know that the gansta life is B.S. Johnson enjoys hip hop music and is a well-known hip hop artist. To see old videos of my music, search Youtube under the Vito Rip Kumoel. He currently incarcerated.

JUAN is a 24-year-old Free Minds Book Club and Writing Workshop member. In 2006, he was arrested and charged as an adult at the age of 16. He served seven years in prison. In addition to playing semi-professional basketball and working full-time as a welder, Juan now serves as a "Poet Ambassador" for Free Minds Book Club and Writing Workshop speaking at community gatherings on the power of creative writing to transform lives that have been traumatized by violence.

TATIANA SHANIQUE LAING is a junior honors student at American University. She is majoring in CLEG (Communications, Law, Economics, and Government) and has a deep interest in reducing mass incarceration by improving reentry practices. In the spring of 2013, Tatiana was selected to become a consulting editor for BleakHouse publishing and became one of the founding writers for BleakHouse's blog, The Bare Lightbulb. Tatiana interned for Brennan Center for Justice, where she gained invaluable experience in advocacy and research about mass incarceration. She hopes to practice law and continue to advocate for racial and criminal justice issues in the United States.

G. LEAKS (No bio provided)

LORENA LIPE is a sophomore at American University. Originally from Brooklyn, NY, Lorena is currently studying Law and Society and plans to attend law school after graduation. She is very interested in human and prisoner rights, having been very involved with Amnesty International.

IAN LUCIANO is originally from Sydney, Australia. He currently is a sophomore at New England College majoring in Criminal Justice.

RICK LYON is the author of a book of poems entitled "Bell 8" that was published by BOA Editions. His work has appeared in print in Colorado Review, The Missouri Review, and The New Republic and online at Poetry Daily. He is a boat captain from Connecticut, originally, now living and working in Chicago and is also working as an RV transporter making deliveries throughout the United States and Canada.

JOHN RALEY is a writer and former jail inmate. While incarcerated, he had three poetry books and one fiction novel published on PrisonsFoundation.org—a website that publishes the written works of men and women behind bars. Raley is also a stage actor and singer and has studied acting in ALL its styles in Washington, DC and New York City. For many, many years he has worked with and for animal rights and welfare organizations.

MIKALA REMPE is a sophomore originally from Omaha, Nebraska studying literature and creative writing. Her poems are her best friends and worst enemies.

JASON RUSSIN (Author) is a second year student at New England College. He lives in Vermont.

ANNE SCHERER is a writer and artist who resides in Rochester, Minnesota. She has been a long time advocate for Peace and Justice issues and currently is pursuing advocacy work with Victims of Abuse. Anne enjoys reading, music, walking and of course writing and drawing. Anne graduated from the University of Wisconsin-Madison with a Bachelors degree in Art with her focus on Drawing and Photography.

DANI SKLARZ is an honors undergraduate studying Film and Media Arts at American University, though her roots are from Greenwich, Connecticut. Daniella is a passionate writer. Most recently, through the help of AU players, she wrote a script to a musical that was performed for an audience. Daniella is involved with Hillel, Women's Initiative, AU Players and is a member of Delta Gamma and Delta Kappa Alpha.

ELIJAHWON WATTS is an 18-year-old Free Minds Book Club member. He is nearing the finish line in his pursuit of a high school diploma. He is a prolific poet. He comes from a large family and loves to play football. Elijahwon's dream is to make his mom proud. He plans to open his own barbershop.

ANTHONY WINN (No bio provided)

www.ingramcontent.com/pod-product-compliance
Lightning Source LLC
Chambersburg PA
CBHW051955290426
44110CB00015B/2245